Frank
the Not-So-Boring
Fish

by Philip Ardagh
Illustrated by Alex Patrick

OXFORD
UNIVERSITY PRESS

Chapter 1
Can fish smile?

Eddie had wanted a dog, but his dad gave him a fish instead. It wasn't even a goldfish. It was a boring grey colour.

"Isn't he great?" said Dad. "The man in the shop said his name is Frank."

Eddie looked at the grey fish and sighed. "Hello, Frank," he said.

Frank GRINNED back.

Eddie's eyes widened in surprise. "I didn't know fish could smile!" he said.

Dad put Frank's fishbowl in Eddie's room. He handed him a tub of fish food.

"Only feed him once a day," said Dad. "You should never overfeed fish."

"OK, Dad," said Eddie.

Just before bed, Eddie sprinkled a few flakes of fish food into Frank's bowl. Frank swam over and swallowed them ALL in one big mouthful.

Frank looked at Eddie with a hungry expression on his face. He pointed at his mouth with a fin.

"More?" asked Eddie, not quite believing what he was seeing.

Frank the fish nodded. Eddie gave him a few more flakes. Frank swam around three times and looked happy.

Can you show a hungry expression, as if you were Frank the fish?

Chapter 2
Feed me

The next morning, Eddie looked at Frank's bowl and GASPED!

Frank had grown so much in the night that he was almost as big as his bowl! His face was squished up against the glass, and he was staring at Eddie with his big fishy eyes.

"Oh no!" thought Eddie. "Maybe I overfed Frank. What will Dad say?" Eddie decided not to find out! He ran to the kitchen.

Eddie opened the cupboard where they kept all the saucepans. He was looking for the REALLY BIG one. He filled it to the brim with water and carried it back to his bedroom.

Eddie carefully tipped Frank from the fishbowl into the saucepan full of water. Frank swam around three times and looked happy.

"Come on, Eddie!" Dad called out. "You mustn't be late for school!"

That night, Eddie gave Frank a few flakes of fish food. The fish gave him the hungry look again, so Eddie gave him a few more.

The next morning, Frank had grown too big for the saucepan!

Eddie kept some of his toys in a big plastic crate. He tipped them out and filled the crate with water. Next, he tipped Frank from the saucepan into the crate. Frank swam around three times and looked happy.

That night, Frank made the 'feed-me-more' expression again.

By the next morning, it had happened again … Frank was almost the size of the crate!

Luckily, it was Saturday. No school! Eddie had a plan.

Chapter 3
A shark in a wheelbarrow

"Dad! I'm going to see Uncle Malcolm," Eddie shouted as he dragged the crate through the front door.

Outside, Eddie carefully lifted Frank into a large wheelbarrow filled with water. He pulled a cover over the top then set off towards town.

"What's under there?" asked a <u>familiar</u> voice.

If something is <u>familiar</u> it means you recognize it. Do you think that Eddie knows the person who is speaking?

Eddie sighed. It was Jenny Norris. She was in Eddie's class at school.

"It's a shark," Eddie lied.

"Liar!" said Jenny. She yanked the cover off the wheelbarrow and screamed. Frank was staring up at her with a VERY impressive set of teeth.

Eddie almost screamed, too! He hadn't realized that Frank even had teeth.

Jenny ran back to her house and locked the door.

"Well, I think you're handsome," Eddie said, pulling the cover back over Frank. He wheeled the wheelbarrow down a long, <u>straight</u> road.

Can you pretend to be Eddie pushing the wheelbarrow down the road? Can you go in a very <u>straight</u> line?

After a while, he arrived at the aquarium.

Eddie pushed the wheelbarrow up the slope and into the building.

Eddie's uncle, Malcolm, worked at the aquarium.

"Morning, Uncle Malcolm!" Eddie said.

"Hello, Eddie," Malcolm replied. "What have you got there?"

"An unusual fish," Eddie replied. "He needs a new home."

Malcolm peered at Frank. Frank grinned back.

"This way," said Malcolm quickly. He led Eddie along a walkway, which ran round the top of the biggest tank. "Put him in there."

Eddie tipped Frank into the water. Frank swam around three times and looked happy.

Chapter 4
Doctor Frank N. Stein

On Monday, after school, Eddie cycled to the shop where Dad had bought Frank.

"I'm here about Frank the fish," Eddie declared.

"Ah yes, Frank," said the man behind the counter. "I named him after myself: Doctor Frank N. Stein."

"Well, he keeps growing!" said Eddie.

"Hmm," said the doctor. "How big is he now?"

Eddie stretched out his arms.

"Oh," said the doctor. "I wasn't sure if he would grow at all, but now he has, I think he's going to get MUCH bigger."

Eddie gulped. "I have to go!" he said, racing outside and jumping on his bike.

When he got to the aquarium, Eddie's eyes almost popped out of his head!

There was a truck outside with a giant glass tank on the back. Frank was inside the tank, looking bigger than EVER! There was also a crowd of people, including photographers and reporters.

When Frank saw Eddie, his face broke into a great big fishy smile. Frank tried to do a loop-the-loop, but he was too big and banged his head on the glass. The whole tank shook from side to side and water slopped over the top.

The crowd gasped as a wave covered them.

The truck started up, and off it went.

Eddie had to pedal like mad to keep up. Luckily, the truck drove slowly <u>throughout</u> the short journey.

They arrived at the local nature reserve and stopped by a beautiful, big lake.

Less than an hour later, Frank was swimming around in the water.

The truck drove slowly <u>throughout</u> the journey. Does this mean it drove slowly for the whole journey, or just for some of the time?

Once the truck had gone, Eddie went down to the water's edge. He called Frank's name.

The fish broke through the surface of the water, gave the goofiest grin and waved a fin.

Eddie waved back. Frank swam around three times and looked happier than he'd ever been.

Eddie went to see Frank every day after that. Sometimes Jenny went with him.

"I've decided that Frank's not so scary after all," Jenny <u>declared</u>.

Eddie ended up changing Frank's name to Frankie, though, because *he* turned out to be a *she*!

How did Eddie know that? Because Frankie had lots of baby fish. They all grew VERY, VERY LARGE INDEED!

To <u>declare</u> something is to say it clearly or firmly. Can you pretend to be Jenny <u>declaring</u> that Frank isn't so scary?

As for Doctor Frank N. Stein and his shop ... it turned out the doctor often found homes for unusual and <u>unknown</u> animals.

That was how Eddie came to own a three-eyed parrot. However, that's another story ...

'<u>Unknown</u>' means something not known or not familiar. Can you think of another way to say '<u>unknown</u> animals'?

Read and discuss

Read and talk about the following.

Page 5: Can you show an <u>expression</u> of anger? What about surprise, or happiness?

Page 11: Can you describe some <u>familiar</u> sounds that you might hear at school?

Page 13: Can you give directions to get from one place to another at your school, using the word 'straight'?

Page 20: What do you think Frank was thinking <u>throughout</u> the journey to the lake?

Page 22: Can you think of a time when you might <u>declare</u> something? Can you <u>declare</u> it in a grand voice?

Page 23: Can you make up a name for another <u>unknown</u> animal? What might it look like?